Teenage Refugees From

CHINA

Speak Out

IN THEIR OWN VOICES

Teenage Refugees From
CHINA
Speak Out

COLLEEN SHE

THE ROSEN PUBLISHING GROUP, INC.
NEW YORK

Published in 1995 by The Rosen Publishing Group, Inc.
29 East 21st Street, New York, New York 10010

First Edition
Copyright © 1995 by The Rosen Publishing Group, Inc.

All rights reserved. No part of this book may be reproduced in any form without permission in writing from the publisher, except by a reviewer.

Manufactured in the United States of America.

Library of Congress Cataloging-in-Publication Data

Teenage refugees from China speak out / [compiled by] Colleen She. — 1st ed.
    p.   cm. — (In their own voices)
Includes bibliographical references and index.
ISBN 0-8239-1847-5
1. Chinese American teenagers—Juvenile literature. 2. Refugees—United States—Juvenile literature. [Chinese Americans. 2. Refugees. 3. Youths' writings.] I. She, Colleen. II. Series.
E184.C5T44 1995
305.23'5'089951073—dc20   94-40368
                                                  CIP
                                                  AC

Contents

Introduction   7

1) Eileen: Bamboo Brush and Inkstone   16

2) Qing Ren: Pizza and Pressure   20

3) Peter: Memories on Tape   28

4) Feng: Grandmother's Noodles   34

5) An Qing: Tea Bricks in Our Luggage   40

6) Mi: Reading *Wuxia*   46

7) Yi-hua: My Father's Mystical Medicine   52

Glossary   60

For Further Reading   62

Index   63

China is a vast and beautiful country with a varied landscape and a diverse population.

INTRODUCTION

Chinese history spans thousands of years. Historians have divided it into dynasties. Each dynasty was ruled by a series of emperors. An emperor was both the symbolic and the factual ruler of China. If the imperial heir was incapable of living up to his responsibilities, there were plenty of ambitious ministers anxious to rule instead. An imperial dynasty might rule for a few years or even decades. Eventually, the dynasty would collapse, because of a war or an economic crisis. Although emperors do not rule China today, the Chinese are still fascinated with their past. Television dramas that romanticize ancient China are extremely popular. These dramas are called *gu zhuange pian* or "ancient costume" shows.

Perhaps you've seen the movie *The Last Emperor*, which depicts the end of the dynastic era. China has now moved into the post-imperial or modern era. The heads of the modern Chinese state are the premier and his cabinet members.

Although the political system in China today is not a democracy, it has come a long way from its ancient imperial past. A great deal of political power is still held by top officials. As the national economy grows, however, and as China is increasingly exposed to the world economy, more people will probably find ways to acquire independent wealth. This economic independence will undoubtedly affect China's political system.

During the 1960s, the Cultural Revolution occurred. This revolution attacked China's roots. Initiated by Chairman Mao Zedong, the Cultural Revolution was an attempt to destroy any trace of traditional Chinese culture. Chairman Mao believed that it was time for the people to rebel against the strictures of ancient society. Many temples and ancient relics were vandalized by an army of brainwashed youths directed by Mao. China's traditional elite, the educated, became targets of criticism and abuse. Most intellectuals were sent to the countryside for hard labor, a crucial part of their indoctrination into Mao's new way of thinking.

The people suffered a great deal during this time and were deeply affected by the events that took place. Some people cannot talk about it to this day. The scars of the past range from physical disability to severe mental illness. This author's grandfather was a member of a political faction that opposed the leaders in China during the 1960s. Many of his relatives suffered by association. His daughter, who is still living in China, suffers from severe

In New York City, a young Chinese immigrant participates in a demonstration for democracy in China.

Free-market economic reforms have encouraged many Chinese to "moonlight" in jobs such as taxi-driving.

delusions because of the deprivation and hardship she endured during the Revolution. In the 1980s, when her family in the United States reestablished contact with relatives still in China, they received many letters from her. In the scrawled muddle of her letters, she revealed many things that had happened to her. Being from the "wrong" family, she was paraded in the street and forced to wear a dunce-cap. She went for weeks with almost no food. She was publicly humiliated. Many people like her suffer for the rest of their lives as a result of the indignities to which they were subjected.

Mao Zedong's actions led to dismal consequences, to be sure. Severe social problems did need to be addressed and perhaps intellectuals represented an easy target. It is difficult to comprehend fully the Cultural Revolution. In fact, historians are still researching the archives that are gradually being opened.

Today, most Chinese living in the United States planned their emigration. They were not forced to leave by war, political repression, or other difficult circumstances. However, one must have a legitimate reason to come to the United States from China. That reason is often education.

Many of the teens interviewed in this book have parents who are students in the United States. People come from all over the world to pursue advanced degrees from the prestigious universities and colleges in the United States. When they obtain their credentials, they can put their valuable knowledge to work in China, although sometimes they choose to remain in the U.S.

Education is an important theme throughout this book. As you will discover, the foremost concern of Chinese teens living in the U.S. is gaining a proper education. Many express concern about living up to the stereotype of being excellent students. Although doing well in school is generally a positive goal, for many it means continuous pressure. A good education is often seen as a means of social advancement. In ancient times, when the emperor appointed his ministers, he chose candidates who had made it through a highly competitive procedure called the palace

Chinese Catholic peasants pray at a popular shrine. China is home to several different religions.

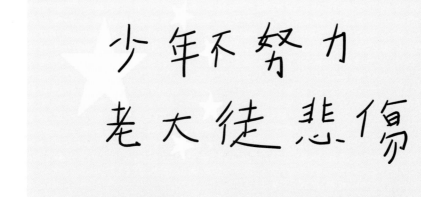

ENGLISH TRANSLATION FROM CANTONESE:
If you do not study when you are young,
you will feel sad when you are older
because you have lost time.

examinations. In reality, these exams tested an individual's knowledge of obscure and difficult books written in ancient Chinese. So much emphasis was placed on the exams that people often resorted to cheating. Failure to pass often led to suicide. Although palace examinations were abolished many years ago, success is still equated with education in Chinese culture today.

Virtually all of the teens interviewed here are excellent students. Through the teachings of their parents, they believe that education is the key to success. They are all college-bound and determined to work hard for future success. To preserve their privacy we have used only their first names.◆

In 1989, thousands of Chinese students and workers gathered in Beijing's Tienanmen Square to call for democratic reforms.

A young Chinese woman makes an emotional speech to her fellow students at the Tienanmen Square demonstrations.

Protest in Tienanmen Square

Tienanmen Square is located in Beijing, China's capital. In May of 1989, students and workers gathered in Tienanmen Square to demand democracy and more freedom. At first, the protests were made up of a small group of students, but in time, many others joined in the demonstrations. As many as a million people stayed in the square to protest the Communist regime. The protests were peaceful at first, but on the morning of June 4, armored troops stormed the square and killed at least 400 civilians. Many students, especially demonstration leaders, were arrested, murdered, or forced to flee China. The international outcry over China's handling of the situation led the Chinese government to adopt more liberalized policies in 1991, although martial law was not lifted in Beijing until 1992.

Eileen is a relative newcomer to the United States. She has lived in Texas, where she is a high school sophomore, for only six months. Memories of her native city, Shanghai, are still fresh in her mind, and she talks in detail about the city and its people. Eileen practices the traditional Chinese art of calligraphy, which requires a great deal of practice. Here is a sample of her work.

EILEEN
BAMBOO BRUSH AND INKSTONE

I am a sophomore at Bellaire Senior High School. My Chinese name is Wei-lai, but to most people here I am Eileen. I came to the United States last year and have lived in Texas for about six months. In China, I lived in Shanghai. The first difference I noticed between China and the United States was the population density. China is teeming with people. Another thing that struck me was how many automobiles there are here. In China, most people still rely on bicycles to get to work. I now know that China can truly be defined as a developing country, whereas the United States is already highly developed in its science and technology.

Let me tell you a bit about Shanghai, especially Pu Dong, or East Shanghai. Pu Dong is the newly developing area of Shanghai. The old part of the city has reached its maximum growth. For the

past three years there has been much new con-
struction in Pu Dong, including two massive bridges,
Yang Pu and Nan Pu. According to the government,
many projects are still to come. There is also the
big sewage line. All this planning and preparation
has created a very nervous environment. Shanghai
will most certainly prosper from these develop-
ments. The people of Shanghai are changing the
face of the city and improving the standard of
living for everyone.

Young people in Shanghai like rock stars from
Hong Kong and Taiwan. They enjoy the music so
much that no one ever cares how much a ticket
costs. Due to all the modern influences, Shanghai
kids are dressing more and more like their foreign
friends. In short, young people in Shanghai are
open-minded.

I would like to share with you a very special
hobby of mine. I practice traditional Chinese calligraphy. Not everyone today knows how to write
with a bamboo brush and an inkstone. To excel at
this difficult art takes a lot of concentration. First,
one must make ink by grinding an inkblock against
an inkstone, adding just the right amount of water.
The texture and consistency of the ink must be
just right; otherwise it will run. In ancient times,
the Chinese even bred a kind of monkey that stood
about five inches tall and was trained to stand on
the calligrapher's table and grind ink. I am not
kidding! After the ink is made, you roll the brush
around in it, giving all the fibers a generous drink.
Brushes come in many sizes and shapes. The

Rice paddies are a familiar feature of the Chinese rural landscape.

calligraphy must be done very quickly, as the ink dries in an instant. There is no room for mistakes. Although I have come to the United States and go to an American school, I intend to keep practicing calligraphy.◆

Qing Ren has lived in the United States for four years. He describes the pressure he feels to succeed in school. He attributes this partly to stereotypes of Asian-Americans and partly to his parents' high expectations. His goal is to be a great athlete and to become, as he puts it, "totally Americanized." He believes that it would be difficult for him to go back to living in China at this time in his life.

Qing Ren remembers being in China during the demonstrations in Tienanmen Square in 1989. His recollections reflect the conflict and confusion in China during that time.

QING REN
PIZZA AND PRESSURE

I came to the United States four years ago from Nanking, China. Nanking is less densely populated than many other Chinese cities. It's kind of suburban, with spread-out buildings and wide streets. When I left, the people of Nanking were just starting to build high-rises. My friends tell me that there are McDonald's and KFCs now. For most people in China, eating there is trendy. It proves you have money.

I went to a public school in China. It was a drag because from the sixth grade onward all you were supposed to care about was testing into a good secondary school and then a good high school. Students learn a lot more in China. I had both algebra and geometry by the time I was in eighth grade. Technical training begins early. The humanities are not considered as important. The stress is definitely on math and science because parents want their children to become scientists. **21**

Many large American cities, such as New York, have Chinatowns, communities where Chinese have lived for many years.

Scientists make more money; at least, that was the trend when I left Nanking. Now people are turning more to business ventures such as trading. My uncle trades heavy industrial materials. He has an import-export business.

I guess when a country has been impoverished too long, the first thing people want when the economy starts to grow is wealth. Although some people may view the business craze in China as a festival of greed, imagine if, for the first time in your life, things could actually be your own, and your profit did not have to be turned over to the government. A lot of business people these days are blinded by money. Factories and regular citizens are at fault for ruining the environment. Factories spew chemical waste into rivers without hesitation, while people dump human waste. In many cities, the streets are covered with litter. People get used to dirt and do not have much sense of civic pride.

I don't know if the Chinese people will ever think of themselves as coming together in one mass. During the Tienanmen incident, I happened to be in Shanghai getting a visa to come to the United States. I heard people saying that the students deserved our support. The news reports in China claimed that the government was not doing anything wrong. My mother, who was already in the States, said that the government was not telling the truth.

My immigration to the States has been relatively smooth. I made a real effort to learn English. In my first two years here, I felt lost and alienated. It was so difficult to understand what everyone was saying. Now I consider myself half-Americanized. I eat pizza and other American foods. I like the U.S. a lot better than China. If I went back now, I would never be able to catch up in school.

It is a myth that all Chinese students are perfect. A lot of pressure was put on us at school. I remember in seventh grade my friends and I wanted to try smoking. Just as in American schools, you certainly are not supposed to smoke. We tried some cigarettes at my house. We accidentally left one on the couch and it burned a tiny hole in the upholstery. My dad found out, and we were reprimanded. I found out that smoking was not exciting at all. In fact, it did not feel good. It was not a wise idea.

I am getting ready for college now. I have applied to two state universities. I wanted to apply out of state, but I missed the application deadlines. Mom wants me to major in engineering. I can't think of anything else I would be more interested in.

I hate being under pressure. When I feel pressure, I just can't study. There are times when I don't do my homework. In my school, some parents pay their kids for getting good grades. My mom objects to it. She says, "Don't compete like that." Although she tells me not to compete, sometimes she compares me to her Chinese friends' kids. If kids are good, parents love to boast about them. When Mom can't think of anything good to say

President Richard Nixon made a historic visit to China in 1972, where he met with Communist Party Chairman Mao Zedong.

about me in front of her friends, she keeps quiet.

Mom feels alienated at work. When she has to write reports, she feels she is making a lot of grammatical errors and she doesn't like that. I guess that explains why she doesn't force me to speak Chinese. She thinks I will always remember my native language, but I think I am forgetting it. I want to become totally Americanized. My friends are mostly Americans and Asian-Americans. I want to be a great athlete. Asian guys are discriminated against in sports because they are small.

Some of my American teachers believe that the Chinese are all good at math. That is not true. I think the stereotype comes from the exposure Asian students get. In my school, the Asians often

The bicycle is a common mode of transportation in China.

win Westinghouse scholarships, a college prize for science and technology. People forget that many Asians do not fit the stereotype.

Immigration totally changed my life. If I had stayed in China, I wouldn't be going anywhere now. When I found out I was going to immigrate to the United States, I just stopped studying—I got out of the rat race. Life is easier, at least right now. I miss my friends, though.◆

Peter lives in Minneapolis, Minnesota. A compassionate person and an animal lover, he recalls how he and his friends rescued and cared for stray dogs in his native province of Hunan. Peter has many hobbies, including painting, drawing, gymnastics, and reading. He would like to be an architect someday. His artistic ability is evident in his painting of the Great Wall, below.

PETER
MEMORIES ON TAPE

My name is Peter and I have lived in Minneapolis for four years. I was born in Changsha, Hunan. Dad came to the United States as a student and the rest of my family followed a few years after. I was really excited about coming to the U.S., but my friends in Changsha didn't share my feelings. I admit, I was a little sad as well. The airplane ride was fun.

My favorite thing to do in Hunan was rescuing stray dogs. It is illegal to feed them, but my friends and I took care of dogs and even trained them. Many Chinese people are mean to dogs, because they are supposed to be the lowliest of creatures. I have seen people actually kick and hit dogs. There are not many dogcatchers in China because it is not a public priority. The dog catchers in China do not drive around in big vans like they do here in the United States. They ride bikes or motor-

Poverty is an acute problem for millions of Chinese peasants.

cycles. I heard in the news that kids often get bit-
ten by rabid dogs in China. People there just don't
care about animals as much as they do here. A
dog is a pet here, whereas in China it is just an
animal.

I guess I am lucky, since I grew up around animals. My grandparents have a farm on the outskirts
of Changsha. We had a lot of dogs and chickens.
We had a good time in the countryside catching
frogs. Grandma scolded us when we got dirty. My
grandpa brews wine and beer, which are pretty
expensive and hard to get. His wine is well known
to the people of his village. Grandpa said that I
was too young to help make the wine. He usually got
two very strong men to press the grapes between

wooden boards. It was hard work.

Even though I studied a lot, I played a lot too. I like to draw and paint. I started when I was five. My parents sent me to art class after school. When I was seven, I entered a contest. I did not win anything, but that is okay. Winning is not every-thing. My favorite things to draw are Trans-formers. My parents like to take me to the art museum.

Dad came to the United States before we did. He saved up enough money so that our family could afford a television set while we still lived in China. It is hard for people to get TVs in China unless they have a lot of money. One set might be worth months and months of work. On TV in China, you can see "Chip and Dale." They dub it into Chinese. Chipmunks sound cute in Chinese. I was pretty popular to begin with in my school. I liked to help my classmates with their homework. When we got the television, I became the most popular person in my class. After school, my classmates would squeeze into our apartment to watch television.

I like gymnastics. In China, I went to gymnastics class. These days, I try to do pushups and situps every day. Some kids in China don't get enough exercise. All they do is study. The athletes I most admire are Wayne Gretsky, Shaquille O'Neill, and Joe Montana. Although I like sports, I realize that education is pretty important. My mother keeps on asking me what I want to do for a career. I say, "Why are you asking me about a career now? I am not even close to college age." Mom complains about how much work there is to do in the United States. Sometimes she talks endlessly about this.

In my spare time, I like reading adventure and humor. I have a different sense of humor from my parents. Chinese people do not think canned laughter is at all funny. When my parents watch an American sitcom and hear canned laughter, they just stare blankly at the screen. They don't think throwing a pie in someone's face is funny. But I remember once, on "America's Funniest Home Videos," they laughed hard when a guy's pants fell down at a wedding ceremony. Chinese people tend to laugh where there is shame in-volved.

Modern technology has really touched our lives. Last year, Dad went back to China for a visit. I begged to go with him, but he said, "You must not interrupt your studies." He bought a Camcorder to tape my mother, my sister, and me. We did not know the camera was on. My sister and I started to fight over who should go first. When my dad played it for my grandparents in China, they thought it was funny. They laughed at first, but then they began to cry because they missed us so much. They got a kick out of our messy room. They said we were lazy. In China, Dad taped my grandparents and my cousins. When we saw the tape, I felt a bit sad. My mother cried.

When I grow up, I want to be an architect, but Mom says, "Be a lawyer or a doctor." Chinese parents worry about practical matters quite a bit. I

Chinese President Jiang Zemin is greeted by French President François Mitterand. China has been increasing its dealings with Western countries in recent years.

don't want to be a lawyer because if you put a crazy man in jail and he gets out, he might try to get revenge. I certainly could not be a doctor because I hate the sight of blood.

The purpose of immigration is to work hard and to improve your life. Maybe that means getting a good job. When I look back at pictures of my days in China, I feel melancholy. I remember friends the most.◆

Feng describes the intensity of the Chinese educational system and the fierce competition it creates among students, speculating that perhaps the less rigid structure of education in the U.S. produces more creative students. A major fan of Chinese cooking, she would rather eat home-cooked noodles than pizza any day.

4

FENG
GRANDMOTHER'S NOODLES

I was born in Kunming, the capital of Yunnan province. Like most cities in China, Kunming is densely populated. I began elementary school at the age of five, because both my mother and father had jobs that took them far from home. School was the only place where I could be supervised. You might even say that I was reared in school. I was always, therefore, younger than my classmates.

School was much more difficult for me than it had been for my parents. When they were growing up during the Cultural Revolution, their teachers did not push them. These days, only about one out of ten of us have even the slightest chance of going to college. Ever since I was in elementary school, I have been geared to climb the academic ladder. Success in junior high gets you into a good high school, and likewise, success in high school gets you into the best college. I know it is somewhat the same here in the United States, but at least here you can redeem yourself at any point along the line. If you don't do so well in junior high, you might have a better chance in high school.

For me, the worst part of my education in China began in junior high school. We were crowded into classes of 60 students, elbow to elbow in a dimly lit room. Left-handedness was discouraged because it would limit the places you could sit. In China, they arrange you by height. The tall people always sit at the back of the classroom. It is very regimented. Everybody wears uniforms, and teachers are always making sure your hair is regulation length. The girls have to wear their hair in a very short bob called *xi gua pi*, meaning "watermelon rind."

I miss many things about my homeland, especially the food. I absolutely hate cheese. Chinese people do not eat dairy products. We get our calcium from other things like greens and pigs' feet. One of the specialties of Kunming is fresh rice noodles. I remember that every day vendors would go door to door peddling these noodles. My grandmother made the tastiest recipe. She boiled the noodles with meat and chives until the noodles were swimming in a delicious broth. I don't know if I'll ever come to like American food.

Kunming is called the "Spring City" by the Chinese because the climate is so mild. People say it is similar to California's weather. I never needed more than a sweater all year round. I lived in a beautiful valley at the foot of a mountain range.

Chinese Fried Rice

In a large pot, bring to a boil four cups of water. Add 2 cups of rice, and cover. Turn off the heat. Let the covered pot sit on the stove for 30 minutes. Test to see if the rice is as done as you like it. For softer rice, add more water, turn heat on low, cover the pot, and allow the water to evaporate. Be careful not to let the rice burn. In a large frying pan, brown one pound of hamburger meat. Add 2 tablespoons of soy sauce and salt and pepper to taste. Put meat into a mixing bowl and let stand. Scramble two eggs in 2 tablespoons of vegetable oil. Set aside. Stir-fry mushrooms, green onions, and any other vegetable you wish to add. Pour everything into a large bowl and mix together. Season with soy sauce.

I used to gaze at Western Mountain, part of a range that captured the imagination of Kunming locals. We could all see the form of a beautiful lady sleeping peacefully on the horizon. The climate there has worsened over the years, because of human destruction of the environment, I believe. One of our most beautiful lakes was dammed up during the Cultural Revolution. Many factories now spit out pollutants into the once-beautiful waters. We have acid rain, which is called *suan yu* or "sour rain" in Chinese. If the price of economic development is environmental ruin, I often wonder if it is worth it.

I like my high school in the U.S. I think American students are very creative. In China, we are not supposed to think for ourselves. There is a saying you hear a lot from the older generation: "Good children will study without complaint." We were

STUDYING HARD THE FOUR MODERNIZATIONS

A Chinese peasant woman stops for a break under a billboard encouraging students to study hard.

taught only to memorize what the teachers lectured. Never, never do you question what a teacher has to say. If you question them, you are just asking for a slap on the palm with a ruler. This is not considered abusive in China.

In the United States, I had a difficult time in school at first because I had been taught British English in China. Nobody could understand me if I said I wanted to meet them "ofter" school. Everybody here says "after" in a flat nasal tone. One time a classmate asked to borrow my eraser. I did not know what was wanted; in England they call an eraser a "rubber." So I just kept on giving my classmate everything I had until I got it right. My teachers are so nice, though. I don't feel afraid to ask them questions. Chinese teachers criticize you if you ask them questions.

Although I miss my friends in Kunming, I love being with my parents. I have only been here six months, so I have a lot ahead of me.♦

An Qing is from Mongolia. Mongolians are one of many ethnic groups that make up China's diverse population. Mongolians have their own language and culture. In the early thirteenth century, the Mongols became a major force under their ruler, Genghis Khan. His son, Kublai Khan, later conquered China. An Qing describes some aspects of Chinese discrimination against Mongolians today.

5
AN QING
TEA BRICKS IN OUR LUGGAGE

I come from Hohhot, the capital city of Inner Mongolia. Inner Mongolia is considered part of mainland China. It has an interesting mixed culture of Mongolians and Chinese. About ten percent of the people speak purely Mongolian. Mandarin Chinese is the predominant language in most schools. I went to a special Mongolian school for most of my elementary education, so I can speak both Mongolian and Chinese. Outer Mongolia is independent from mainland China. The ethnic Mongolian people lead a nomadic lifestyle. Most of the major cities of Outer Mongolia are inhabited by the ethnic Chinese.

Although I spent most of my time in the city of Hohhot, my parents have spent time in the Mon- **41** golian countryside. During the Cultural Revolution, many intellectuals and Chinese elite were targeted by the government and forced to do hard labor in the countryside. Many people from other regions of China had a horrible time when they were sent to the countryside, but my parents said many of the country people were extremely friendly.

Although many Mongolians are settling down to cultivate land these days, when my parents went to the countryside during the 1960s, most Mongolians were still nomads. They let their livestock graze freely on the steppe, and when an area was grazed clean, they moved on to another fertile area. Mongolians are meat and dairy consumers, unlike mainland Chinese. They eat lamb and beef as a staple. They make a special kind of sour cream butter.

I come from an ethnically mixed background. My grandmother was Manchurian and my grandfather was Mongolian. Grandfather was an important official, a Wang Ye (pronounced hwang yeh).

When we first came to the United States, we had some unusual things in our luggage. We brought *cha zhuan*, or "tea bricks" with us. Tea bricks are made from the dregs of tea production, congealed into a large block. The tea brick is definitely a vestige of Mongolian nomadic culture. It makes the tea easier to transport than if the leaves were loosely packed. A block lasts about a year and a half. To brew Mongolian tea, you chip off a part of the block and add a generous portion of goat's milk and salt. Yes, salt, not sugar. The salt helps fend off dehydration when you are out all day on horseback.

Dad is the second person in the entire Mongolian region to have a Ph.D. I am lucky to have the opportunity to pursue my education in the United States. When I was in Mongolia, life was very simple—go to school and study hard. I lived with my grandparents when Dad came to the U.S. to study in 1985. In the cities of Inner Mongolia, language is a kind of social barrier. The official language is Chinese. If you don't speak Chinese, people may not do business with you. My parents wanted me to study Mongolian because they did not want me to be snobbish. They said they had met many goodhearted Mongolian people in the countryside and hoped that I could always communicate with them. After fourth grade, I changed over to a Chinese school, largely for practical reasons.

In order to emigrate to the United States, my sister and I had to go to Beijing. Before we could get into the U.S. embassy to apply for a visa, we had to go to our local police department in Hohhot to get an entry permit. When we were interviewed by the immigration officer in the embassy compound, he asked, "Why do you want to emigrate to the U.S.?" My sister and I, being a bit naïve, responded, "Because we want to see our parents." Needless to say, we were denied our visas. We attempted two more times, to no avail. The immigration officer was not going to let us go to the United States just to see our parents. They thought we would just turn around and come back after a great effort had been made to get us there.

On the fourth attempt, my dad talked to the officer, who was finally convinced. I don't remember having been particularly excited about going to the U.S. My dad emerged from the interview room joyfully and proclaimed, "I got your visa!" Without much of a change in my tone, I responded, "Okay, great." At that time, the immigration officer's suspicions were correct. I intended to go back to Mongolia in six months. I even brought my books from school, thinking that I would not let myself get behind. Well, obviously I did not return to Mongolia. I like it here now.

In the United States, you have a chance to get a good job with decent pay. Under the Chinese system, you cannot choose your occupation. The government selects people to engage in certain occupations. My dad always wanted to become a physicist, but the government wanted him to study agriculture, so that is what he did. I want to become an electrical engineer. There is no reason to study hard unless you know in what direction you are headed. I will probably go to a community college for two years and then transfer to Colorado State University.

My parents are happy that they immigrated to this country, but they have not forgotten their homeland. Dad wants me to join the Peace Corps so that I can see just how good a life I have. Dad says that you learn through comparison. There is always someone less fortunate than yourself. My dad wants to retire in China because he feels a great debt to his country for sponsoring his edu-

Population in some areas of China, like the city of Shanghai, is extremely dense.

cation. Although many people come here to further their education, they miss friends and family in China. There is a sense of camaraderie that is lost in the United States. Even so, I guess we are lucky to be here.♦

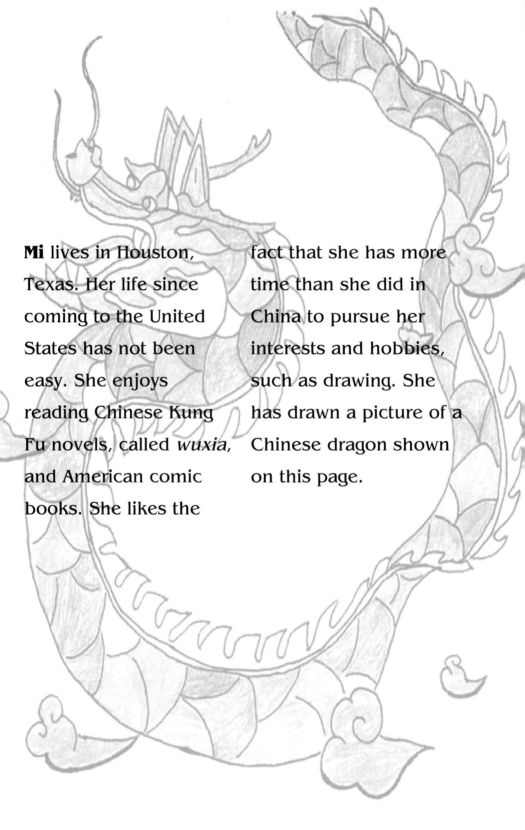

Mi lives in Houston, Texas. Her life since coming to the United States has not been easy. She enjoys reading Chinese Kung Fu novels, called *wuxia*, and American comic books. She likes the fact that she has more time than she did in China to pursue her interests and hobbies, such as drawing. She has drawn a picture of a Chinese dragon shown on this page.

6
MI
READING *WUXIA*

What I recall most about Shanghai is a pervasive nervousness among students. In China today, though there are regional differences in lifestyle, all teenagers must face the same social pressure of excelling in school. We started class every day at 7:30 in the morning and did not finish until 5:30. In China, students don't move from class to class. Instead, they stay in one classroom while the teachers move around. In this way, you tend to bond with your classmates. The relationship of *tongxue* (pronounced tong shooeh) or classmate solidarity can be lifelong. Even as adults, you still remember the bonds you formed in school.

Life has not been all that easy for us in Houston. Although there is a large Chinese community, we've had to face many family hardships without much outside support. Houston has a large Chinatown, but it is quite isolated, and my family certainly **47**

Chinese refugees attempting to enter the United States by boat face inspection by an immigration officer off the coast of San Francisco.

is not much a part of it. We live in a nice neighborhood. My father is pursuing a degree in physics. My mother was a materials scientist in China. Unfortunately, she is unable to work or pursue studies now because she has a terminal illness. It seems to be in remission now. When she started to feel ill, we went to some Chinese doctors, but they were unable to determine what was wrong with her. Finally, she went to Western specialists here in Houston. She seems to be getting better. We will just take things a day at a time.

My parents are quite liberal. They have lived in the cosmopolitan culture of Shanghai. Many

foreign businesses establish their branch offices

in Shanghai. So, as a Shanghainese, you are far more worldly than people from other parts of China. Before World War II, Shanghai was called the Paris of the East. My parents really like fine arts. I myself am interested in comics, especially "Tom and Jerry," which is syndicated in China.

We also have a comic based on an ancient Chinese classic about the Monkey King. Once upon a time there was an orphaned child. Somebody put him in a raft and set him free to drift to a faraway kingdom. The raft was discovered by a monk, who adopted the orphan. Eventually, the orphan became a monk and had a burning desire to go to the Western Heaven to seek the Tripitika, a sacred Buddhist sculpture. On the way he met Guanyin, the Chinese goddess of mercy, who told him he would encounter 99 disasters from which he could be saved by only four beings. Among the four beings, one was the Monkey King. The adventures encountered by the monk and the Monkey King are the subject of a comic strip in China. I think Chinese comic strips tend to be educational, not funny, which is why I prefer "Tom and Jerry."

Young people in China love to read *wuxia* (pronounced wu shah) novels by Jin Yong. These novels describe the adventurous lives of the Kung Fu masters and their nearly miraculous feats and death-defying challenges. I love novels by Chong Yao. She writes about romance in a very emotionally intense way. Sometimes she describes the conflict felt by lovers in an arranged marriage. There is usually a third lover involved, the true love that can never be had. Even though arranged marriage is not practiced formally in China today, parents still have a strong say in their approval or disapproval of a marriage. The psychological pressure is very real. My teachers in China used to say, "You are far too young to be reading Chong Yao novels!"

Shanghai is a bustling city. Most young people don't care about politics as much as they care about fashion and culture. I think Beijing is a rather provincial city, even though it is the center of politics. I am used to a city where there are many things within my reach. I like Janet Jackson and Whitney Houston. There are also pop songs in China. Many times the artists come from either Hong Kong or Taiwan. Chinese pop stars are clean cut and wear sporty, fashionable clothes. They have a lot of influence on what we like to wear. When I left Shanghai, hats were all the rage. Long T-shirts were in as well. Women in China like very feminine clothing. They like to look cutesy and childlike. Sometimes you see women riding bikes in lacy dresses and high heels. They manage to get around somehow.

I like being in the United States. Life here is good. Because pressure from school is less than it was in China, I have time to do things I enjoy. One of my favorite things is video games. I stay up way past my bedtime in front of the television set.♦

McDonald's opened its first restaurant in China in 1990 and is an example of a new Chinese openness toward Western influences.

Yi-hua is from Beijing and comes from a family where Chinese medicine has been passed down from one generation to the next. Her father was allowed to emigrate from China because he helped to cure a prominent official in the Communist Party. Yi-hua's parents met during the Cultural Revolution.

7

YI-HUA
MY FATHER'S MYSTICAL
MEDICINE

I was born and raised in Beijing, China. I have only been in the United States for three months. My immigration here was planned by my parents. I have been separated from them for nearly ten years. It is difficult to come to a strange land and live with parents you did not grow up with. I feel that getting reacquainted with my parents will be my greatest challenge.

My maternal grandmother practically raised me. She took care of my every need and tried in every way to be a substitute parent. It was hard for her to let go of me, but she must have known that she could not keep me forever. Because Dad makes good money here in the States, our whole family has been well provided for. In Beijing, I lived in an apartment with my grandparents. Grandmother told me that before the Cultural Revolution, my mother's side of the family lived in a courtyard-

In Beijing, workers from the countryside wait for word of new jobs.

style house. Most of these houses have now been torn down and replaced with high-rises.

I come from a family of doctors. My maternal grandparents both practice Western medicine. My father's side of the family have been Chinese doctors for several generations. The art of Chinese medicine has been passed down to my father, who is a licensed acupuncturist. I am growing closer to my father with each passing day. He lets me help him in the office on weekends. He says, "One day you might be able to go back to China to study Chinese medicine." I think he hopes that I will carry on the tradition.

Dad has studied Chinese medicine since he was a child. He apprenticed with my grandfather, starting by learning how to determine a person's health by feeling the pulse and looking at the tongue. I can help Dad prepare some of the simple herbal remedies he prescribes. Under his strict supervision, I am learning how to select the right herbs in the right amounts. Of course, he does all the serious work, like acupuncture. If I tried to poke people with needles, I might hurt them!

In helping my father, I have learned that he has a great sense of humor. He likes to joke around with his patients. One time a woman patient asked him if he could make her younger. Dad said, "Younger, no; better, yes." He manages to get his point across, even with his heavy Beijing accent. He draws out his "r's"—like "betterrrr."

When I grow up, I want to be wealthy. I love cars and can't wait until I am old enough to drive. When Dad first came to the States, he did not have a car. He rode a bicycle everywhere. I am not fond of exercise. I don't know how he managed. My parents say that I don't appreciate how difficult it was for them to get started. Dad never could imagine that anyone here would be willing to try Chinese medicine, so he started out by working as a janitor in a restaurant. One day, a worker hurt his back and Dad was able to treat him. Gradually, through word of mouth he started to have a practice—in the kitchen of his tiny apartment. He did not know at the time how strict the zoning laws are in the States. In China, business and residential areas are not differentiated. People just set up shop where they feel like it. Needless to say, his neighbors started to complain. He did not know what to do. Because he was a likable man, and an apparently effective doctor, his patients rounded up enough funds for him to set up an office.

My father's life is like a fairy tale. My parents met during the Cultural Revolution. They helped each other out during those difficult years. My mother came to the United States first. I am not sure exactly why. My father remained in China and missed my mother a great deal. There was virtually no way they could see each other. The government was afraid that if husband and wife were together in the U.S., there would be no incentive to return to China. That was the policy during the early 1980s. It is better now.

You would never believe how my father came to the U.S. in the first place. He was given the chance to perform the "miracle" of a lifetime. A

積极开展119防火安全宣传月活

Mao Zedong, former chairman of the Communist Party, is depicted in many statues and billboards around China.

During the Tienanmen Square demonstrations, protestors burned copies of the official Communist Party newspaper.

high-ranking Communist official was ill. He had been treated by Western doctors, but he remained very ill. My father then tried his hand at curing him. Actually, it was not really a miracle. Chinese medicine is a rational, not a mystical discipline. The official was not cured overnight; it took about a year. For this favor, my father was granted his wish, to visit his wife in the United States.

I owe my immigration to my parents. It is what they have strived for all these years. Now that we are together, a new chapter in each of our lives is just beginning. Sometimes I feel pressure on me to do well in school. Mom worries that I will not be able to catch up in English class. Dad's American patients tell her not to worry because there is ESL and a variety of programs in school to help me get on my feet. I say, English is one thing, making friends is another. Because Dad is so busy and Mom does not like to drive, it is hard for me to visit schoolmates on the weekends. I wish I could.♦

Glossary

acupuncture Chinese medical practice of puncturing parts of the body with fine needles in an effort to cure disease or ease pain.

bonding Relationship that grows between parents and newborn child or between people who are thrown closely together for long periods.

culture The beliefs and traits common to a racial, social, or religious group.

dynasty Series of rulers of the same descent who succeed one another without interruption.

environment The totality of one's surroundings, including air, water, and other physical conditions.

humanities Study of literature, language, art, and philosophy, as opposed to sciences.

indoctrinate To teach a particular ideology, especially under pressure.

intellectual Person of superior mental capacity and education.

repression Process of placing a person or group of people under subjection.

stereotype Standardized opinion, usually demeaning, held about a group or race.

vandalism Deliberate destruction or damaging of public property.

For Further Reading

Anderson, Eugene N. *The Food of China*. New Haven: Yale University Press, 1988.

Asia Watch Committee. *Freedom of Religion in China*. New York: Human Rights Watch, 1992.

Barlow, Tani E. *Chinese Reflections: Americans Teaching in the People's Republic*. New York: Praeger, 1985.

Barnouin, Barbara. *Ten Years of Turbulence: The Chinese Cultural Revolution*. London: Chapman & Hall, Inc., 1993.

Chin, Ann-Ping. *Children of China: Voices from Recent Years*. New York: Knopf, 1988.

Kingston, Maxine Hong. *The Woman Warrior*. New York: Knopf, 1990.

Tan, Amy. *The Joy Luck Club*. New York: Putnam, 1989.

Theroux, Paul. *The Great Railway Bazaar: By Train Through Asia*. Boston: Houghton Mifflin, 1975.

Index

A

acid rain, 37
acupuncture, 55
An Qing, 40-45

B

brainwashing, 8
building boom, 18

C

calligraphy, 16, 18-19
career, choosing, 31, 32, 44
Chinese medicine, 55
Chinese, speaking, 25
classmate, bonding with, 47
comic strips, 47
Cultural Revolution, 8–11, 35,
        37, 42, 53, 56
culture, Chinese, 8
cure, "miracle," 59

D

dogs, rescuing, 29-30

E

Eileen, 16-19
emigration, planned, 11, 53
English

British, 39
learning, 23-24, 59
environment, damage to, 23, 37

F

Feng, 34-39
food
    American, 24
    Chinese, 36, 37
    Mongolian, 41

G

gymnastics, 31

H

high-rises, 21, 55
Hohhot, 41, 43
Hong Kong, 18
humor, Chinese, 32, 55

I

illness, mental, 8-10
Inner Mongolia, 41
intellectuals, Chinese, 8-11, 42

L

language barrier, 43

languages
   Chinese, 41, 43
   Mandarin Chinese, 41
   Mongolian, 41, 43

M
Manchurian, 42
Mao Zedong, 8, 10
Mi, 46-51
music, popular, 18, 50

N
Nanking, 21
nomads, 41-42
novels, Kung Fu, 49

P
palace examinations, 11-13
Peace Corps, 44

Q
Qing Ren, 20-27

S
school
   in China, 21, 35-36, 43, 47
   in Mongolia, 41
   in U.S., 37-38
Shanghai, 17-18, 47
stereotype, Asian student, 11, 25-26

T
Taiwan, 18
tea bricks, 42
television, Chinese, 31
Tienanmen Square, 15, 20

W
Western medicine, 55

Y
Yihua, 52-59

Acknowledgments
Thanks to Gina Ng for additional research.

About the Author
Colleen She is a first-generation Asian-American. She grew up in Colorado, fascinated by stories her parents recounted about their harrowing escape from mainland China during the late 1940s. She studied history at the University of California– Berkeley and East Asian languages and cultures at Columbia University. She now works with American companies, helping them to publish marketing literature in Chinese and Japanese.
   Ms. She lives in Southern California.

Photo Credits
p. 14, 15, 16 © 1989 Khiang T'ang (Cuon Tran), Impact Visuals; all other photos © AP/Wide World Photos

Layout and Design
Kim Sonsky